Venerable Philip

A Brief Sketch of the Life an... ... .……..

of the Society of the Sacred Heart in America

G. E. M.

Alpha Editions

This edition published in 2024

ISBN : 9789362929839

Design and Setting By
Alpha Editions
www.alphaedis.com
Email - info@alphaedis.com

As per information held with us this book is in Public Domain.
This book is a reproduction of an important historical work. Alpha Editions uses the best technology to reproduce historical work in the same manner it was first published to preserve its original nature. Any marks or number seen are left intentionally to preserve its true form.

Contents

PREFACE. ....- 1 -
CHAPTER I ....- 2 -
CHAPTER II ....- 6 -
CHAPTER III ....- 9 -
CHAPTER IV ....- 13 -
CHAPTER V ....- 16 -
CHAPTER VI ....- 20 -
CHAPTER VII ....- 23 -
CHAPTER VIII ....- 25 -
CHAPTER IX ....- 29 -

PREFACE.

There have been many heroic figures in the history of American Catholicity. The sowing of the faith in our beloved land was not accomplished lightly. Anguish of soul and weariness of body were required of our pioneers, no less than of those of other lands. Our predecessors in this portion of God's vineyard left home and kindred and friends and cast themselves on a strange shore, wanderers for God's cause, giving their lives in labor and anguish of spirit, that the glad tidings of salvation might be spread far and wide.

Some of these folk were martyrs in very truth. Through the mercy of Christ their heart's blood has sanctified our soil. Others by living their length of days in the midst of privations and sorrows, that Christ might be known and glorified, fell little short of the martyrdom of blood itself. The memory of these still lives, enshrined in hearts that love them for their tireless zeal and their dauntless courage. Of such pioneers was the Venerable Philippine Duchesne, a truly valiant woman, to whom the American Church owes a debt of gratitude too great for payment.

The following pages are too few to give more than a glimpse of her heroic labors, but they have caught inspiration from their subject, and something, too, of her fragrant piety. No one will read them without admiration for one who was so weak and yet so strong, so humble, and yet so daring in work for God.

Mother Duchesne has a lesson for this age of softness and indolence. She has shown us the way to heroism and offers us motives for entering thereon. For this gratitude is due. This sketch is conceived in a spirit of thankfulness, a tribute of appreciation that will speak a clear, forceful message to sad hearts and selfish hearts and timorous souls, inspiring all with great ideals and holy ambitions to do a mite for the leader, Christ.

R. H. T.

CHAPTER I

VOLUNTEERS FOR THE AMERICAN MISSIONS

In the early annals of the Catholic Church in this country, no name stands more preeminent than that of the Venerable Philippine Duchesne. She was one of the first, and altogether the greatest, among the spiritual daughters of the Blessed Madeleine Sophie Barat, so well known as the Foundress of the Society of the Sacred Heart. The pioneer of that Institute in the New World, it was in the midst of sorrow, and penury, and strenuous toil, that she cast the seed of the harvest whose plentiful sheaves are carried with joy by those who have come after her. She was a valiant cooperator in the work of the Catholic missionaries during the early part of the last century, and American Catholics can scarcely fail to be interested in her story.

She was born in Grenoble, France, August 29, 1769, the same year as Napoleon Bonaparte. Her father, Pierre François Duchesne, was a prosperous lawyer, practising in the Parliament, or law court of Grenoble, the capital of the Province of Dauphiny, while her mother, Rose Perrier, belonged to a family of wealthy merchants of the same city. Pierre François Duchesne had adopted the false teachings of Voltaire and his school, but his wife was very pious, and carefully brought up her children in the love and fear of God. Philippine was the next to the last in a family of six. From her earliest years she was noted for her serious turn of mind. One of her chief pleasures was reading, but even this had to be of a serious kind. Roman history was an especial favorite, but what she loved most of all was the lives of the saints, particularly the martyrs. Another of her pleasures was to assist the poor. All of her pocket money, with everything else that she could dispose of, went to them, and she loved to distribute her alms with her own hand.

At the age of twelve she was placed as a pupil at Sainte Marie d'en Haut, the Visitation Convent of her native city, to be prepared for her first Holy Communion. The remarkable spirit of prayer, of which she had given very early evidence, developed itself here, and her happiest moments were those she was permitted to spend in adoration before the Blessed Sacrament. A diligent and conscientious student, so ardent was her piety, that she was allowed by the kind nuns the privilege of making her morning meditation and reciting the Office in choir with them. The year after her admission into the school she made her First Communion, and it was on this happy occasion that she heard the call to a perfect life. Her parents, suspecting what was in her mind, removed her from the Convent. She silently acquiesced in this decision, keeping her own counsel, and continuing her studies with great success, in company with her cousins, the young Perfiers, who were afterward at the head of a great banking business in Paris, under the rule of the first Napoleon.

After four years of patient waiting, in the hope of obtaining her parents' consent, and convinced at last that they never would grant it, she decided that it was time to act, and entered the novitiate of the Visitation. Her family became somewhat reconciled to her choice, after striving in vain to induce her to return home; but when the time for her profession came, her father absolutely forbade her to make it, on account of the dangerous political conditions of the time.

Four years later, in 1792, when the revolutionary storm was at its height, religious communities were being everywhere expelled from their homes, and Monsieur Duchesne withdrew his daughter from her convent, which was soon converted into a prison, and went to reside with his family in the Chateau of Granne, situated in a retired part of the country. By this time all her sisters were married, except the youngest, a child in her 'teens; and when her mother was overtaken by her last illness, she it was who cared for her with devoted affection, and finally closed her eyes in death. After this the family possessions were divided among the children, and Philippine surrendered her share to the others, reserving only a small pension, barely sufficient for her needs.

This business being settled, she removed to a modest apartment in Grenoble, in order to be able to devote herself to works of mercy. Her ardent charity and intrepid energy found a wide field of action in those calamitous times. She visited and succored the unfortunate victims doomed to the guillotine, with whom the prisons were crowded. She ministered to the sick, and sought in their hiding places, the devoted priests who would not abandon their posts, to bring them to the bedside of the dying. She did all this at the constant risk of her life, often hearing sounds and witnessing sights that made her shudder with horror. As soon as the revolutionary storm had spent its fury somewhat, she was enabled to turn her attention to the neglected boys she found in the streets, assembling them in her own lodgings to teach them to read and write, and above all, to prepare them for the Sacraments.

At last, when the advent of Napoleon to power restored political and social order, Philippine Duchesne who, during all these years, had considered herself as irrevocably consecrated to the service of God, observing the rules and customs of the Visitation as closely as the adverse circumstances of the time would permit, resolved to reestablish in their old home the surviving members of the community of Sainte Marie d'en Haut, and resume a religious life with them. She obtained possession of the convent through the influence of her cousins, the Perriers, but her attempt to reorganize the community was not successful. In the meantime, however, several companions had gathered around her, forming a little community with the title of "Daughters of Faith," under the direction of the Vicar General of Grenoble, the Abbé Rivet. This was in 1803 and the following year.

In the meantime, Madame Duchesne had heard, through the Abbé Rivet, of the Society of the Sacred Heart recently founded by Mother Madeleine Sophie Barat, under the guidance of Father Joseph Varin. It was through the latter that she applied for admission into the new Society. Father Varin, in reporting the case to the holy Foundress, declared that Madame Duchesne was a soul worth seeking for even to the end of the world. Lack of space does not permit us to dwell upon the beautiful humility, submission and childlike docility this valiant woman displayed in her intercourse with her new superior, who was ten years younger than herself, or her joy at finding herself under religious discipline and obedience. Nor can we stop to describe her heroic devotedness, zeal and charity toward all; her incredible activity, her self-immolation, the wonderful spirit of prayer that held her motionless the livelong night before the Tabernacle, when holy obedience allowed her the privilege.

The ten years that followed her profession were spent at Sainte Marie d'en Haut, toiling with an unflagging energy vivified and made fruitful by her intimate union with God. It was during that interval that the death of her father occurred. In his last illness, she surrounded him with the most loving care, and had the consolation of bringing him back to the faith of his baptism, and seeing him atone for the errors of a lifetime by a sincere repentance and an edifying end.

In the depths of her heart, Mother Duchesne had felt from the first an intense longing to devote herself to the evangelization of the barbarous tribes still sitting in darkness and in the shadow of death; but hitherto she had not seen any opening in that direction. So she was patient and put out her hands to all the strong things that Divine Providence placed in her way. One day, however, the illustrious Dom Augustin de Lestrange, Abbot of La Trappe, visited Sainte Marie d'en Haut, on his return from a tour among the North American missions. It was on the feast of Pentecost, a circumstance that did not escape the piety of Madame Duchesne; and the account he gave of the labors, dangers and fatigues endured by the missionaries in the New World, communicated a new and almost uncontrollable intensity to her apostolic yearnings. After this, she was possessed by one thought and one desire, that of devoting herself to the conversion of the savages of America. A few days later, she wrote to Mother Barat to tell her of Dom de Lestrange's visit and of the ardent desires his discourses had aroused in her heart for the missions of America in particular. Mother Barat was delighted, but insisted that she must school herself to patience, until some providential opening should offer. For this she waited twelve long years, but with what burning desires, what tears and prayers! It would take too long to relate the circumstances which led to the visit of Mgr. Louis Valentin Dubourg, the newly consecrated Bishop of Louisiana, and describe the touching scene, when Mother Barat, in presence of the humble yet ardent entreaties of her strong-souled daughter, recognized the will of God, and gave the consent she implored, to let her have a share in the missionary labors of the zealous prelate in the far-off region of Louisiana.

In the hearts of God's saints, joy and sorrow are in close alliance. Mother Duchesne was overwhelmed with joy on seeing the realization of her ardent and long-cherished desires; but a midnight blackness settled upon her soul, when she found herself about to sail away from the shores of sunny France, leaving behind her all that her loving heart held so dear, and with the conviction that the parting was final, as far as this life was concerned. But her strong spirit did not flinch for an instant, and the world would never have known how keenly she felt the sacrifice, were it not for a few lines in one of her letters to Mother Barat. Her companions were Madame Octavie Berthold, a fervent convert, whose father had been secretary to Voltaire; Madame Eugénie Audé, a young lady whose grace and elegance had been admired at the court of Savoy, and two lay sisters of tried virtue. After a tedious voyage of ten weeks in a small sailing vessel, they reached New Orleans on the Feast of the Sacred Heart, May 29, 1818, and as soon as it was possible, they set out for St. Louis in one of the primitive steamboats of the time, a trip of six weeks, with numberless inconveniences and a very rough set of fellow-passengers.

CHAPTER II

FIRST SCHOOLS IN THE NEW WORLD

Mgr. Dubourg cordially welcomed them to his Episcopal city, but the best he could do for them was to assign to them a log-house, which he had leased for their use at St. Charles, a village on the Missouri River, at a distance of thirty miles from St. Louis. Here they opened a boarding school which at first was only very scantily attended. They also opened a school for poor children, which immediately gathered in twenty-two pupils. As the nuns could not afford to keep a servant, they themselves had to cultivate the garden which, when they arrived, was a wilderness of weeds and briars. They also had to care for their cow and milk it, to chop wood for their fires, to bake their bread, to do the cooking and washing, besides teaching the two schools. For their supply of water, they were compelled to depend upon the muddy current of the Missouri River, brought to them in small bucketfuls, for which they had to pay an exorbitant price. The summer was very hot, and the cold of winter was so intense, that the clothes, hung up to dry near the kitchen stove, froze stiff. They had to be careful in handling the tin plates, etc., which served for their meals, lest their hands should adhere to them. The white fingers of Mesdames Audé and Berthold soon became hard and grimy. As for Mother Duchesne her hands had become rugged and horny long ago, from the hard, rough work to which she had devoted herself, especially after her reentrance into Sainte Marie d'en Haut. Indeed, it had always been her custom to reserve to herself, as much as possible, every kind of work that might be most painful or fatiguing for others. These particulars offer but a faint idea of the sufferings and privations endured by these refined and accomplished ladies, during those hard beginnings of the Society of the Sacred Heart in the New World.

During this trying time, Mother Duchesne's desolation of heart was extreme, and her sense of loneliness indescribable. Whatever labors and austerities she had imposed upon herself hitherto, she had always had a circle of friends of the choicest kind and spiritual directors with whom she felt at her ease, but now all this was a thing of the past. Neither did she find any consolation in prayer. Her soul seemed dead within her, and yet, besides keeping up her own courage, she had to sustain that of her young companions, less inured to suffering and without her granite endurance. Still they were very brave and Bishop Dubourg could not but admire the valiant spirit and the cheerfulness of all.

But the establishment at St. Charles was only a temporary arrangement to last for one year; and, as the house that was building at Florissant was not yet ready when the lease expired, Bishop Dubourg gave them the use of his farm near that village during the interval of waiting, with the log house upon it built by the consecrated hands of the bishop himself and of his heroic fellow missionaries. Toward the middle of September, 1819, followed by the intense regrets of the Abbé Richard, Curé of St. Charles, and by the tears of the children of the free school, Mother Duchesne moved to the farm which had been thus placed at her disposal. The boarders, now increased to about twenty, accompanied them to their new home. Here one room and a garret was all that the nuns had for themselves and their pupils; but they had also a poor little chapel, where they were able to keep Him, who was the source of all their strength, and whose presence among them sweetened their life of toil and privation.

Mother Duchesne's presence and supervision had hastened the work upon the new home, that was going up on a piece of ground given to them by the bishop; and by the end of December, it was sufficiently advanced to be habitable. Before leaving the farm, a great consolation was granted to the devoted nuns, in a retreat given by Father de Andreis, the saintly Lazarist missionary, who in 1900 was placed on the list of candidates for canonization. He cleared up Mother Duchesne's perplexities on various points, and between those two kindred souls, there sprung up a holy friendship, which was for her a consolation and a support. Unfortunately, less than two years later, a malignant fever carried away this great servant of God, in the midst of his fruitful apostolic labors.

On Christmas Eve, the removal to the new house took place. Mother Duchesne and Audé were the last to leave the farmhouse, and it was late when they reached their destination, for they had made the entire way on foot, through deep snow, and in the face of a freezing wind. The little community set at once to the work of preparing their small and humble chapel for Midnight Mass, at which nuns and pupils, and also the workmen employed on the house, assisted and received Holy Communion. With regret we find ourselves compelled to pass over many interesting and touching particulars, such as the blessing and encouragement sent by the Sovereign Pontiff then reigning, the saintly Pius VII, and the gift of several relics and pictures from Bishop Dubourg, among the latter one that Mother Duchesne had greatly longed for, that of St. Francis Régis, her special patron, whose name is so intimately connected with her own.

At Florissant, a new field was opened to her charity. Bishop Dubourg's farm was intended by him as a quiet and healthful retreat, where his missionaries might, for a while, rest and refresh themselves after their toilsome apostolic journeys, or when their health required particular care. Madame Duchesne was a mother to them, furnishing them with their meals at any hour of the day, as they dropped in, often three or four at a time, washing and mending their clothes, and replacing them when needful, giving them the best of everything she had in the house. This occasioned a great deal of work and no small expense, and money was very scarce with her, to say nothing of the debts which had been incurred for the building of the house. But this valiant woman counted upon the Providence of God which never failed her, though its gifts were usually bestowed upon her so sparingly, as barely to keep her afloat. It was a great joy to her to help and serve the missionaries, and she declared that she would consider her life happy and well-spent, could she do nothing more than cook their meals for them. This generous hospitality was all the more heroic from the precarious condition of her own finances. Besides the debts, very heavy for the time, which were pressing upon her, and which she had been obliged to incur for the building of her house, a great business depression throughout the country reduced the number of her pupils, thus diminishing the small returns from the school, and, in 1820, a prolonged drought dried up the wells and compelled her to send to the river for all the water they needed.

Toward the end of 1820, when matters began to improve, the community was visited by sickness. Mother Duchesne's turn came last, and so serious was her illness that it brought her to the verge of the grave. She recovered, however, and was able to resume her work at the end of two months.

It was just after this that vocations began to come in. The first were Emilie Saint Cyr, one of her pupils, and the sisters Eulalie and Mathilde Hamilton, of a very distinguished family related to the Fenwicks of Maryland, and also two lay sisters, Mary Layton and Mary Ann Summers. These five formed the nucleus of a novitiate whose numbers increased by degrees.

CHAPTER III

TRIALS AT FLORISSANT

In 1821, the little community of Florissant sent out its first offshoot. With the consent and approbation of her Superior General, Mother Barat, Mother Duchesne made her second foundation in Lower Louisiana, as it was then called, at a place known as Grand Coteau, in the Opelousas region. Mother Eugénie Audé and Sister Mary Layton were sent to begin it. A little later, Mother Duchesne was able to send them valuable help in the person of Madame Xavier (Anna) Murphy, who had just arrived from France with Madame Lucile Mathevon, another valiant woman, who had a notable part to play in the early history of the Society of the Sacred Heart in America.

The school at Grand Coteau had soon filled up, but ere long Mother Duchesne heard of the distressing condition to which the new community was reduced, through sickness and overwork. With the uncalculating charity that characterized her, she at once determined to go in person to their assistance, though it was in the middle of summer and the journey must necessarily be long and painful, as well as expensive. She took with her Madame St. Cyr and a lay novice to leave at Grand Coteau, and Therese Pratte, whose family had so hospitably entertained her and her companions during their two weeks' stay in St. Louis, after their arrival. The young girl was one of her pupils, who had obtained her father's consent for a visit to Mother Audé.

The voyage was long, full of difficulties and endless interruptions and delays, and marked by very dramatic and even tragic incidents, especially on the return trip, of which alone we will give a brief account. Among other particulars, she had to go from Plaquimine all the way down to New Orleans to find a boat for St. Louis. In New Orleans she was stricken with malarial fever, still the physician advised her departure by the first steamer, because at the time yellow fever was epidemic in the city. Scarcely, however, had the steamer started on her voyage, before the dread disease broke out on board, the captain being the first to die of it. Mother Duchesne, though reduced to a state of great prostration, gathered up the remnant of her strength to take care of one of the yellow fever patients on board, to whom no one else seemed to give any attention. She not only ministered to his needs, but converted and baptized him before he died.

Weak and exhausted as she was, foreseeing that under the existing conditions the steamer would scarcely be able to reach her destination, she determined to trust in Providence, and land with her young companion at Natchez. But the quarantine excluded her from the town, nor would any one in the neighborhood take them in, for fear of the prevailing epidemic. Providence came to their assistance, for, as they sat by the river bank upon their trunks, alone and friendless, a young man chanced to pass by, and seeing them so forlorn, offered his services and went in search of shelter for them. Soon he found an honest German who willingly took them in, but he had no bed to offer them, except the one in which his wife had died of yellow fever a fortnight previously, and of which not even the sheets had been changed. From this place Mother Duchesne found means of making her distress known to the Abbé Maenhaut, Curé of the church in the town, and in later years Rector of the Cathedral of New Orleans. He came promptly to her assistance, and had her removed to the hospitable home of a family of the name of Davis. Complete rest and change of air restored her health, and in a few weeks she reembarked for St. Louis on the steamer Cincinnati. On their way up they passed by a steamboat tied up and partially wrecked, in charge of three men. It was the Hecla, the boat from which she had landed at Natchez. Then it was that she could see how providential had been the change she had made. The yellow fever had continued its ravages on the unfortunate boat, and on a little island nearby could be seen the graves of thirteen of its victims. Moreover, the boilers had exploded and several men had been severely injured. At last, after another delay of two weeks, caused by the grounding of the Cincinnati, Mother Duchesne and her companion reached St. Louis, after an absence of five months. The account of this terrible journey contained in Mother Duchesne's letters to Mother Barat is such as might come from the pen of a saint. There is not a word of complaint, and no regrets for herself, save for the Communions and Masses she had lost.

On her return to Florissant she found the school greatly diminished and in a state of insubordination; this latter condition prevailed not only among the pupils, but also among the orphans, of whom she always had several in the house, and whom she educated and provided for entirely. Her firm hand soon reestablished order, but it was not in her power to remove what had been the cause of the state of disturbance, in which she had found the school. The times were very hard; there was little money in circulation, and Bishop Dubourg had been obliged to borrow in order to finish his new cathedral, which the rapid increase of the population rendered necessary. The great bishop's administrative ability was above question, but the resources he had counted upon failed him, through the dishonesty of an agent, and this, with the difficulty of the times, made it impossible for him to meet his obligations; while his creditors, finding themselves in much the same situation, were clamorous against him, breaking out into abuse and menaces. They were even threatening to seize his residence and have it sold for their benefit.

As a matter of course, Mother Duchesne and her community shared largely in the odium that had fallen upon Bishop Dubourg. She was afflicted, but chiefly on account of the indignities offered to the great missionary prelate, and the harm done to religion by the nature of the difficulties in which he found himself involved. After a time the storm subsided, leaving, however, in the public mind a feeling of rancor and resentment, one of whose effects was a settled enmity with regard to Mother Duchesne and her community. Soon, of the pupils left to her, there were only two whose schooling was being paid for. Still her courage and her reliance upon God never wavered, and her confidence was rewarded. She does not say how it happened, but she affirms that she was never less pinched by poverty than at this time. She met this crisis in her usual heroic fashion. Disregarding the idle talk of which she was the subject, she refused to dismiss any of the boarding pupils who were being educated gratis. She already had a free school for girls, and she opened another for boys, as also two classes, one for the poor women of the village and one for the grown-up girls.

And how, with such scanty resources, did she manage to make both ends meet? By her own thrift and ingenious industry, which enabled her to turn the least trifle to account, with an occasional remittance of a few hundred francs from her relatives, and such assistance as Mother Barat could spare out of her own penury. But her surest asset was her confidence in Divine Providence, which always came to her assistance, often in the most remarkable manner. With these she covered the expenses of her convent, extinguished by degrees her indebtedness, and at the same time was prodigal in her charity toward the missionaries, and very liberal toward the poor.

In the situation above described, St. Louis was no place for Bishop Dubourg. Leaving in charge there his newly-consecrated coadjutor, Bishop Rosati, he took up his residence at a short distance above New Orleans. The last of the many benefits he had conferred upon Missouri was a foundation for a little company of Jesuit Fathers and scholastics, to whom he donated his farm at Florissant. They arrived just at this time, and on account of their connection with the prelate met with a cool reception from many of the people. This was another heavy affliction for Mother Duchesne, who felt that, in view of the good they could surely do in the country, neither she nor any one else could do too much for them. Their poverty was very great, and she did not hesitate to beg for them. The friends she still had left in St. Louis responded generously to her appeal, and sent her whatever they could afford to give. From others, however, to whom she had recourse, she met with harsh refusals. She despoiled herself and her community of all she could manage to do without. She took care of the altar linen and vestments for their domestic chapel, and spent part of her nights mending and making clothes for them. In the beginning she sent them their meals already prepared, and later on she supplied them with many articles for their missionary outfit. In fact, the Jesuit Mission of Missouri might have perished at its birth had it not been for her fostering care. It was to her an immense joy to see the abundant fruits the zeal and devotedness of the Fathers soon began to reap in the country around, to the distance of a hundred miles and more. She considered it a priceless benefit to have their Superior, Father Van Quickenborne, as chaplain, and above all, as confessor for the community.

After the coming of the Jesuit Fathers, Bishop Rosati's missionaries seldom made any stay at Florissant, but they were constantly passing through it to and from their missions, and Mother Duchesne continued to keep open house for them as heretofore.

Her apostolic longings for the work of the evangelization of the Indians had never died out, and great was her delight when, one day, Father Van Quickenborne brought her two little Indian girls, shyly hiding under his cloak, and asked her to take them and educate them. This was the beginning of the Indian school which, while it lasted, was the joy of her heart. However, it never counted more than twenty children, and came to an end in two years, the Indians being driven back further and further by the inflowing tide of white immigration.

CHAPTER IV
ST. MICHAEL'S ESTABLISHED

In 1825, Mother Duchesne was called upon for another foundation. Father Delacroix, the predecessor of Father Van Quickenborne, as pastor of Florissant, was a holy and learned Belgian priest, whom Bishop Dubourg used to call his angel. He had the highest opinion of Mother Duchesne's sanctity, and became a lifelong friend of hers. After leaving Florissant, he was stationed upon the Mississippi River, at a considerable distance above New Orleans. Before long, with the approbation of Bishop Dubourg, he asked for a foundation of the Religious of the Sacred Heart in his neighborhood. His petition was readily granted, and a location was chosen in the Parish of St. James. To meet the first expenses of the building, the zealous pastor handed over eighteen thousand dollars, which he had collected for the purpose. This was the house known as St. Michael's. Mother Audé was its first Superior, and soon it was in as flourishing a condition as that of Grand Coteau.

Two years later, 1827, Father Neil, one of the resident pastors of St. Louis and director of the college founded by Bishop Dubourg, asked for and obtained a foundation in that city. This was what Mother Duchesne, as well as Mother Barat, had been wishing for from the very beginning. Moreover, though Mother Duchesne had no idea of giving up Florissant, it was too distant from the city for convenience, and besides various other drawbacks, every rain flooded the convent grounds, greatly adding to the hardships endured by the nuns. She applied to Mr. John Mullanphy, a wealthy capitalist, asking him to sell her one of the houses he owned in St. Louis, and he gave her one, with twenty-four acres of ground on the outskirts of the city, together with some assistance in money, on condition that she would, in perpetuity, keep twenty orphans. The house had the name of being haunted on account of the strange, unearthly noises heard in it, especially at night. That circumstance did not frighten Mother Duchesne, who soon discovered that the ghosts were nothing but cats that dropped down the chimneys to hold their nightly assemblies in the vacant rooms. On the first of May of that same year she took possession of the house with one companion, and remained there as Superior, leaving Mother Lucille Mathevon in her place at Florissant. The following year she had in her charge twelve boarders, ten orphans and forty day pupils, most of the latter having been received gratis.

Here, as elsewhere, her life was one of extreme poverty, privation and unremitting toil, to which, as she had always done, she added fasts, vigils and bodily penances, such as have rarely been equalled in the lives of the greatest canonized saints. She was often without a cent in the house, but this did not prove a bar to her charity. The poor never left the convent door empty handed, and the priests, most of whom were doing missionary work, and were as poor as herself, became the objects of her particular care. She supplied them with clothes, especially cassocks, that they might make a suitable appearance at the altar, and also altar linen and vestments, which she embroidered and made herself. During the first year of her stay in St. Louis, her greatest privation, for herself and her community, was the lack of spiritual assistance. On week days they were often without Mass, and on such occasions Mother Duchesne would remain fasting until noon, in the hope that some priest might drop in to offer the Holy Sacrifice at a later hour, as it sometimes happened, or who at least, might give her Holy Communion.

In the meantime, the Jesuit Fathers had been making great headway, and they acquired a firm footing in St. Louis, when Bishop Rosati handed over to Father Van Quickenborne, the head of the newly-organized Mission of Missouri, the college founded several years previously by Bishop Dubourg, and which, in the course of time, developed into the present St. Louis University. But Father Van Quickenborne was replaced some months later in the office of Superior by Father Verhaegen, who had come with him from Maryland in 1823. In this same year, 1827, the latter founded a permanent mission at St. Charles, and made it his headquarters. He also established, at the same place, a school for boys, and applied at once to Mother Duchesne to found one for girls. It seemed a rash undertaking to make two foundations in the same year, with such scanty resources in subjects and money; but what tempted her was the spiritual destitution of the people, who were all Catholics, and among whom the Protestants were busily at work. Mother Barat, tempted in the same way, gave her consent, and Mother Lucille Mathevon was placed in charge of the new house. It did a great deal of good, in spite of a long struggle with poverty and adversity.

Just a little before this time, at Bishop Rosati's desire, Mother Duchesne, with Mother Barat's approbation, had taken charge of the house of the Daughters of Charity, founded by the Father Nerinckx, near the head of the Bayou Lafourche, in the present State of Louisiana, and now threatened with extinction for want of vocations. The devoted prelate's earnest request could not be refused, but the foundation was an unpromising one from the beginning, and a few years later it had to be closed.

The following year, 1828, as there were already six American houses, Mother Barat directed Mother Duchesne to assemble their superiors in a Provincial Council, in order to take measures for securing uniformity of action among them; and, to spare them the trouble of coming to her, Mother Duchesne went down to meet them at St. Michael's. After the Council she visited the houses in Louisiana, and was able, in her report to the Mother General, to give a very favorable account of them all except that of Lafourche where, to say nothing of other obstacles to success, the directions given by her in accordance with the intentions of Mother Barat, had not been understood or carried out.

CHAPTER V

SERIOUS CROSSES

God's saints have never been spared the cross of contradiction, and Mother Duchesne was no exception to the rule. Mother Barat heard from various persons that she was too austere, too narrow, too unwilling to adapt herself to the requirements of the times; and this, it was said, was why the houses in Missouri were not progressing. By these critics, their backwardness was contrasted with the flourishing condition of the Southern houses. There were numerous reasons for this difference. Louisiana had been colonized a century earlier; its people were wealthy and prosperous; nearly all spoke the French language, and as yet there was little or no competition; whereas entirely opposite conditions prevailed in Missouri. Mother Barat, however, heard these charges so often that she began to fear they were true, and to consider that it was time to place the government of the St. Louis house, at least, in the hands of a younger superior, who would have a clearer understanding of the needs of the times. But before taking a step which was very much against her inclination, she consulted Bishop Rosati, in 1832. His answer was that the removal of Mother Duchesne from her office would result in the collapse of the houses in Missouri, as there was no one else capable of bearing the burden of governing them; that the slowness of success for which she was blamed, was due to difficulties inherent in the situation, while her recognized sanctity gave her an influence for good that no one else would wield. This was not Mother Duchesne's opinion of herself. On the contrary, she thought herself an encumbrance and a drawback upon God's work; and again and again, ever since she had been in America, she had begged to be replaced by some one who would possess the virtues and abilities in which she thought herself entirely lacking. Bishop Rosati's reply was a great relief to the heart of Mother Barat, and Mother Duchesne remained in office for the time being.

The years immediately following brought the holy Mother many crosses, of which we can only name the most notable. Mother Régis Hamilton, the dearest of her American daughters, had to undergo a severe operation, according to the rude surgical methods of the time. The ravages of the cholera in France filled her with anxiety for the fate of the French houses, as also for that of her own relatives and friends, and letters were long in coming.

The cholera broke out with great violence in St. Michael's, where it carried away five of the community, and finally it reached St. Louis. One morning, after her brief rest, she arose to find every one in the community ill except herself. Happily the disease had appeared among them in a milder form, known as cholerine. No one died, but during three months all the sick suffered from continual relapses. The devoted Mother seemed to multiply herself to be able to attend to them all, and at the same time to look after the house. Often she was up the whole night with those who were the more seriously affected. Fortunately, the orphans were spared, and so were the houses of Florissant and St. Charles, but Mother Duchesne heard, with great desolation of heart, that besides the five religious already mentioned, the pestilence had carried off her old friends, the Abbé Martial, Mgr. de Neckere, first Bishop of New Orleans after the division of the diocese, and twenty priests--an immense loss to the Church and to souls.

She had been compelled to dismiss all her pupils except the orphans, and was consequently obliged to borrow from the bank to meet ordinary expenses. Under the pressure of so many sorrows and trials, Mother Duchesne determined to appeal to Heaven by a day of fasting and penance, ending with an expiatory procession. She and the older orphans made it barefoot and with a rope around their necks, in the old medieval fashion. A few days later all the sick were well, and the following week she was able to reopen the school. Another great sorrow was the intense sufferings of Mother Octavie Berthold, one of her first companions, whom a cruel malady was now hurrying to the grave, and who died a holy death in November of that same year. During these years, likewise, she heard of the closing of her beloved convent of Sainte Marie d'en Haut, in Grenoble, while at the same time there was question of closing those of Florissant and St. Charles. Under the weight of these crosses and many others, her affliction was indescribable. In a letter to Mother Barat she gives vent to the anguish of her soul, and with touching humility expresses the fear that her sins are the cause of so many calamities.

But Mother Duchesne was too heroic a soul ever to be discouraged. She set herself to work anew with unflinching fortitude, and went on with the building of an addition to her house. The next year, 1834, had opened prosperously with thirty-two boarders, when the cholera broke out afresh, and the bankruptcy of several business houses in St. Louis reduced their number to one-third. Just at this time Mother Audé was called to France, and received orders to visit all the houses before leaving, that of St. Louis included. A few months later Mother Duchesne was removed to Florissant, while Mother Thieffry took her place at St. Louis. We may mention here that the new Superior did not find a way of overcoming the difficulties of the situation, and several years more went by before the St. Louis house entered upon an era of prosperity.

Mother Duchesne resumed her old life at Florissant--a life of prayer, toil and self-immolation. She could be seen engaged in the hardest labor of the house, the stables and the grounds, cooking, washing the dishes, scouring the kitchen utensils, chopping wood, working in the garden with hoe and spade, like an industrious field laborer, sweeping and cleaning in the house, and, in fact, taking upon herself, according to her invariable custom, all that was hardest and most repulsive to nature. She took care of the sick herself, and would let no one else sit up with them at night, on the plea that the others needed their rest more than she did. She took entire charge of the sacristy, which, like the care of the sick, was for her a labor of love. She made the morning call and night visit, directed the different schools, and took a share in the teaching. Her correspondence was usually done at night, and it was also at that time she made up her accounts and prepared the church for great feasts. During the night, likewise, she spent long hours in prayer, in her usual motionless attitude before the Tabernacle. Her thoughts were all upon God, and her prayer was unceasing. When returning from Holy Communion a nimbus of light was sometimes seen around her head. The mere sight of her recalled the presence of God; her intercessory power was universally recognized, and her words had a wonderful efficacy for strengthening, consoling and enlightening souls.

Her hands were rough and hard, like those of an old farm laborer, and in winter time they were swollen, cracked and bleeding with chilblains. To avoid offending the eyes of the children, she used to wear, during the cold season, mittens which she made of scraps of calico or other stuff, sewed together so as to cover them only on the backs, and thus leave them free for work. She wore the same clothes in winter as in summer; her habit was so patched with different shades of black, that the original material could not be distinguished; her shoes were made of pieces of old carpet, and everything that she made use of for herself bore the stamp of her love of poverty, and gave evidence of her contempt for all that the world loves and seeks after. In fact, she presented an appearance which, in others, would have seemed grotesque, but which in her inspired veneration and awe. The pupils wondered and looked upon her as a supernatural being. They were very fond of her, and when they caught sight of her during their recreation hours, they flew to meet her like a flock of birds, and were delighted when they could offer her the least service.

For her scanty meals she gathered up the scraps and leavings from the children's refectory; and wherever she lived at any time, she would have no other cell than the closet under the stairs. Her mattress was barely two inches thick, and she was never known to have any other covering for her bed but an old funeral pall. She ruled the children with a firm hand, but with the affectionate solicitude of a loving and prudent mother. She trained them to be strong Christians and lovers of duty. Those of her pupils who were called to move in the higher ranks of society, were noted, not only for their prudence and Christian reserve, but also for their refinement and distinction of manners and language. The poorer children came in for an equal share of her kindness and care, and her motherly solicitude followed them after they had gone forth into the world. She had warm friends among the most notable families of St. Louis, but Mother Duchesne was no respecter of persons, and the poor were equally welcome, even more so, perhaps, to her time, her counsels, her prayers, her sympathy, and her services.

CHAPTER VI

MISSION TO THE POTTOWATOMIE INDIANS

She had been six years at Florissant when Mother de Galitzin arrived as Visitatrix of the American houses. One of Mother Duchesne's first petitions to her was to be deposed from her office of Superior, on her usual plea of her total unfitness for it. To the sincerity of her estimate of herself, her letters to the Mother Foundress bear ample testimony. In one of them, for instance, she affirms that she was of the nature of a servant, "and," she adds, "it takes more than that to make one fit to govern others." Mother de Galitzin granted her request, and sent her to St. Louis to take her place in the ranks as a simple religious. The Superior of the house, Mother Eleonore Gray, was one of her former novices. Here, for the first time in her life, and to her intense mortification, one of the best private rooms in the house was assigned to her, and she was treated with all the respect and deference due to her. It was a heavy trial to her to be waited upon so continually and attended to so carefully, especially as it interfered with her dear practices of poverty and penance. However, her stay in St. Louis was not long. Early in the year 1841, she had a visit from the great Jesuit missionary, Father de Smet, whom she loved as a most dear son, while he revered and loved her as a mother. One of the first things he always did, when the needs of his missionary work brought him to St. Louis, was to visit his holy friend; but this time he had a special object in view. He wanted a foundation of the Religious of the Sacred Heart among the Pottowatomie Indians, whom the Jesuits had lately taken under their care. This was for the heroic Mother Duchesne like the blast of a trumpet for a warhorse. Her apostolic zeal was ablaze in a moment, and her longing to work among the Indians was as ardent as when she listened to the discourses of Dom de Lestrange, just thirty-five years previously, day for day; for the Father's visit took place on the Feast of Pentecost.

Mother Duchesne's eloquent appeals, with those of Father de Smet, prevailed with Mother de Galitzin and the Superior General. The foundation was decided upon; and likewise, though after much hesitation, Mother Duchesne, in compliance with her eager desire, was allowed to be one of the foundresses. She was seventy-two years old at this time, and suffering from many and painful infirmities, but nothing could dampen her ardor; and Father Verhaegen, when consulted about her going had said, "Let her come, even though we should have to carry her upon our shoulders. Her prayers, her mere presence, will draw down the blessing of Heaven upon our Mission." The four foundresses were Mother Duchesne, Mother Lucille Mathevon, who was to be the Superior, another choir religious, and a Canadian lay Sister, who had had some experience in dealing with Indians. The whole party was under the leadership of Father Verhaegen.

The Pottowatomies testified their joy at the arrival of the little missionary band by going out to meet them in gala attire and in all their war paint. The great red circles around their eyes gave them so ferocious an expression that the nuns were seized with terror, except Mother Duchesne, who was beaming with joy, like a mother meeting her beloved children after a long separation. The task of the nuns was not an easy one. They had to live at first in a hut which one of the Indians had vacated in their favor, and to manage without the most elementary conveniences of civilized life; for, grateful as their new charges were, they had not yet been reclaimed from the ways and habits of savage life. Her companions experienced a certain revulsion of feeling during the first few days; but Mother Duchesne herself was in the joy of her soul, because she was among her dear savages, and because of the poverty and exceptional hardships and repulsiveness of her surroundings, which responded to one of the most powerful attractions of grace in her soul. In fact, she had never before enjoyed so much sensible consolation, except, perhaps, at the time of her admission into the Society of the Sacred Heart.

She had hoped to take her share in the work of the little community, and she even set herself courageously to the task of acquiring the language of the Pottowatomies, but she only succeeded in learning a few words and phrases. These, however, served her in good stead during the winter, which was severer in those days than it is now. The poor Indians were as heedless and as lacking in foresight as children, and did not know how to take care of themselves. Many of them fell sick of throat and lung diseases, and nearly one hundred of them died, in spite of the best efforts of the Fathers and the nuns. During this time Mother Duchesne was very assiduous in her care of them, visiting them in their miserable huts, assisting and consoling them in their sufferings, and helping them to die piously. At the same time she prayed ardently for these dear children of her heart. They were touched beyond measure and would have laid down their lives for her. To give expression to their gratitude and admiration, they offered her the best things they could find--living birds, which they trapped, meat from their hunting, dried pumpkin, ears of new corn, when it was in season, and eggs from the nests of the prairie hens. They were delighted when they could offer these gifts to the "Great Queen of the Great Spirit," as they called her. The other nuns were "Queens of the Great Spirit," she was the "Great Queen." But they also had another name for her. They were struck with her appearance in prayer, and impressed by her intense recollection and the length of time she devoted to it. As her weakness increased so that she was compelled to give up her active work by degrees, she prolonged her prayer, spending many hours every day before the Blessed Sacrament, in her well-known motionless attitude. The Indians seeing her thus were filled with awe, and looking upon her as a being more than human, they called her by a name which meant "the woman who always prays." They would steal up to her, and kneeling down they would reverently kiss the hem of her dress, and then withdraw as noiseless as shadows, fearing to disturb her communings with the Great Spirit. Mother de Galitzin found her very much prostrated when she visited the mission, in the spring of 1842, but seeing her so happy where she was, she had not the heart to remove her. Four months later, however, Bishop Peter Richard Kenrick, Coadjutor of St. Louis, having arrived there for his pastoral visitation, and finding her so exhausted, declared that to leave her there would be to condemn her to a speedy death, and resolved to take her back with him. This was the matter of a heroic sacrifice on her part, especially as she herself did not realize its necessity; but seeing that his mind was made up, she obeyed with a good grace. He took her to St. Charles, where she was welcomed with great rejoicings; but her Indians never forgot her, and the religious who went later to share in the labors of the mission, could bear testimony to the veneration in which she was held among them. Nor did she lose any of the interest she had always felt in them. She continued to pray for them, appealing especially in their favor to her great patron, St. Francis Régis. Moreover, she used all her influence in obtaining supplies for the mission, sending them clothes and bed quilts, which she made herself, as also whatever suitable articles of piety were given to her by her friends.

At St. Charles, Mother Duchesne had the consolation of finding the office of Superior held by Mother Régis Hamilton, the dearest of the daughters she had trained in the way of perfection. She could no longer do any hard work as of old, but she employed her remaining strength in the service of God and of the community. She presided at the studies of the children preparatory to their classes; she taught the catechism to those of the servants who were without proper religious instruction, and prepared them for the sacraments. She was often seen engaged in the lighter household labors, and even in the garden when the weather was favorable. Long after her death the nuns could point out the trees she had planted with her own hands. We have already mentioned her occupation in making quilts for the Indians, and the same service she rendered also to the orphans of the St. Louis house. Her spirit of mortification showed no decrease as she grew in years. Indeed, it seemed to have reached the limit of possibility even from her youth, and Mother Hamilton wisely refrained from interfering with habits which, through long practice, had become a second nature. Many pages might be filled with touching anecdotes illustrating her regularity, humility, obedience, zeal, and all the religious virtues she practised in so heroic a degree. She spent, as usual, long hours in the chapel in prayer; and on Sundays, Feast-days, First Fridays, and all Exposition days, she scarcely left it at all. So notable was her assiduity that the people of the town designated her as the "Sister of the Blessed Sacrament." Here also she was sometimes seen with a supernatural light forming a halo around her head, or shining upon her face.

CHAPTER VII

AFFECTION FOR MOTHER BARAT

Her life, to all outward appearances, flowed on quietly enough at St. Charles, but it was marked by several heavy crosses. The one which caused her the bitterest affliction, and weighed upon her longest was the suspension of Mother Barat's correspondence. It began at the time of her return from the Pottowatomie Mission, 1842, and lasted until 1847. Her letters, all but one, reached Mother Barat; but the first two written after her arrival at St. Charles having remained unanswered, she thought herself in disgrace with her Mother General, to whom she had always been so tenderly united, and did not venture to write again except on one or two important occasions. The silence of Mother Barat, or the suppression of her letters to Mother Duchesne, if it really took place, is a mystery which will probably never be explained. The Superior General had no reason for displeasure against her old friend and one of her dearest daughters; nor was there any one, either in the Mother House or in St. Charles who could have any motive for intercepting her letters, or was capable of conduct so unworthy and so cruel. The motive which led Mother Duchesne to write to Mother Barat in 1843, and again in 1846, was to save the houses of St. Charles and Florissant from the suppression with which they were threatened. The former escaped, but the latter was closed, to the great sorrow of the holy mother, who grieved not from personal motives, but because of the loss it would entail upon the poorer people of the town, since it was the only Catholic school in the place. From the beginning the house of Florissant had been scarcely supporting itself; and Reverend Mother Cutts, the Vicar, thought it better to close it, and so strengthen the other two communities.

In 1847 a business affair required Mother Duchesne to write to the Mother House. This time, not venturing to address Mother Barat in person, she directed her letter to one of the Assistants General, who was well known to her; but her anguish of soul was too keen not to find expression in it. The kind heart of the Mother General was filled with sympathy and compassion; and as she was about to send to America, Mother Aloysia Jouvé, a niece of Mother Duchesne, she directed her to go to St. Charles immediately on arriving, in order to comfort her aunt by her presence. At the same time she made her the bearer of a letter full of the warmest affection. Mother Duchesne's joy and gratitude were in proportion to the bitterness of her past sorrow, and for the remaining years of her life, her correspondence with her beloved Mother General was all that her faithful heart could desire. The latter often sent her presents, which she knew the aged Mother would be happy to bestow upon the other houses, or upon the Indians, or upon the poor.

During the latter years of her life, many of her most valued friends, both in France and in America, passed into their eternity, among others Father Van Quickenborne, and Bishops Dubourg and Rosati, with whom, during so many years, she had borne the heat and the burden of the day, in the harvest field of her Missouri mission. Several times, also, during those years, she was tried by severe illness, to say nothing of the infirmities which overtook her after her arrival in America, and caused her a great deal of suffering without impairing her wonderful activity or inducing her to relax either in her austerities or in her devotions. As she advanced in years, though growing naturally weaker, she was never idle for a moment. When not on her knees in the chapel, she was busy knitting, seated with a prayer-book open before her, in her narrow cell, which to her great consolation, was separated from the chapel only by a partition wall. Sometimes, when the weather was fine, she would go and sit under an old pear-tree in the garden with her knitting. This she would lay down now and then to take up her French hymn book, and with a weak and quavering voice, she would sing the beautiful hymns she had always loved. One of them, entitled "Beau Ciel," was her favorite, for it gave expression to the longing of her soul for her eternal home.

CHAPTER VIII

LAST DAYS

Her dear Mother Régis Hamilton, whom she had found as Superior at St. Charles, on her return from the Pottowatomie Mission, was replaced three years later and sent to Canada. The aged Mother missed her greatly, and when Mother Barat asked her at a later period, what she could do to give her pleasure, she begged for the return of Mother Régis, though, with her usual disinterestedness, it was for the benefit of the community rather than her own, that she desired it. Her petition was granted, and on New Year's Day, 1852, it was with great joy and consolation that she welcomed back her beloved daughter. Mother Régis was pained to find her venerable Mother so worn and weak; but the joy of the latter on having her dear Mother Régis with her again, together with the tender and tactful care with which she was surrounded, restored her strength to some extent and probably prolonged her life for a while.

Two other consolations were given her at this time. She learned that Mother du Rousier was coming to the United States as Visitatrix, and that Father Verhaegen, who for twenty years had had all her confidence, was come to St. Charles as resident pastor. During the following summer she was seized with a violent fever which, though soon broken, left her so debilitated that it was thought prudent to anoint her. The next morning, with her usual energy and fortitude, she wrote three letters; one to Mother Barat, another to her sister, and a third to Father de Smet. She realized that her end was now very near, and she longed for the moment that would unite her to the God she had so ardently loved, and so faithfully served during the whole of her long career. But she awaited the call with the utmost patience and serenity of soul. She still spent a great deal of time on her knees, after her usual fashion, before the Tabernacle, where she was now and then taken with a spell of weakness. Those who happened to be at hand would help her out, but as soon as she had recovered she would return to her prayer as before.

To the last Mother Régis Hamilton was a ministering angel to her, rendering her all the personal services, that nothing but her weakness and exhaustion would have induced her to accept. She lived, as it were, in an atmosphere of peace, gratitude and love, humble, simple and docile as a little child. Faithful to her habits of mortification, she would not consent to have a fire lighted in the little stove that had been placed in her room, even when the chilly autumn days had come.

On the 17th of November, Mother du Rousier arrived, after traveling in great haste over a long distance, and by very bad roads. Their meeting and the long and intimate communication that took place between these two holy souls was a great consolation to both, and a source of light and strength for Mother du Rousier in her great mission of foundress of the Society of the Sacred Heart in South America. A little combat of humility terminated the interview, each claiming a blessing from the other, and considering that it was not her place to give hers to any one so far above her. The touching contest ended in a compromise, and together they blessed each other. Then after exchanging their profession crosses, they parted, looking forward to a future meeting in the realms of the Blessed. Twenty-eight years went by before that happy meeting took place.

Mother Duchesne had taken to her bed only the day before the greatly desired visit, and no one thought that her release was so immediately at hand. For this reason it was that Mother du Rousier, who had interrupted pressing business to hasten to her bedside, left the same day, November 17. The following night the venerable patient was very restless. She could not sleep, but kept repeating prayers with acts of faith, hope, charity and contrition. Early in the succeeding forenoon, Father Verhaegen came to give her the last Sacraments and the indulgence *in articulo mortis*. She continued to sink visibly from hour to hour, but kept again and again repeating her prayers with the greatest ardor until exhaustion would compel her to stop. Then she would murmur expressions of gratitude for the charity of Mother Hamilton and the community. Finally, she remained for a considerable time perfectly calm and united to God, whispering once in a while the ejaculation, "Jesus, Mary and Joseph, I give you my heart, my soul, and my life." At last, at noon exactly, on November 18th, 1852, her pulse ceased to beat, and all was over.

The Religious felt that in her they had lost a treasure of holiness, a shining model of the most heroic virtues, and they could find consolation only in the thought that, in her also, they had henceforth a powerful protectress in Heaven. The news of her decease spread rapidly throughout St. Charles and the surrounding country, profoundly stirring all hearts. "The Saint is dead!" "Oh, what a loss for us!" were the exclamations heard on all sides. The Religious and pupils who, with great emotion, knelt in prayer about her remains were struck with the look of celestial serenity and happiness upon her features. Mother Hamilton, convinced that she would one day be canonized, wished to preserve her portrait for posterity. The only artist in the place was a Mr. Le Faivre, who was in the last stages of tuberculosis and confined to his bed; but such was his veneration for the holy Mother, that he had himself dressed and carried over to the convent in an armchair. There he took the ambrotype picture of her which is still extant, and then he was carried home again to die a few days later.

The funeral took place on the 20th, and was attended by a vast concourse of people from St. Louis, St. Charles, and all the country around. Mother Hamilton, having still in view her future canonization, buried her, not in the common cemetery, but quite near the church adjoining the convent, and upon the slope of the low hill on which it stands. Some time after the crowd had dispersed, a poor woman whom Mother Duchesne had often assisted in many ways, came running to the house full of joyful excitement. Her story was soon told. She had lingered weeping and praying near the new-made grave, when suddenly she had thought of asking Mother Duchesne to intercede for her, that she might be freed from an inveterate and incurable malady that had been tormenting her for years. No sooner had she uttered her petition than she was instantaneously and completely cured. Many other cures and graces of various kinds similarly obtained, contributed to confirm Mother Duchesne's reputation for heroic sanctity, and to inspire confidence in her intercession.

Three years after her death, there was question of opening a street through the convent grounds. This would have separated from the house the spot where the holy religious was buried. Mother Jacquet, who was then Superior, determined to remove the precious remains to a little oratory to be built quite close to the entrance from the street in front. When the grave was opened, the lid of the cedar coffin was found to be in a decayed condition, and the coffin itself was full of mud and water; but the body was so perfectly preserved that every feature was recognizable, and an ambrotype could again be taken, October 23, 1855. This first exhumation was rendered more memorable by a signal occurrence, which caused a great sensation in the general public. This was the cure of a Mrs. Anne King, who was suffering from a cancer that had already eaten away a considerable part of her face. The application of a relic of Mother Duchesne caused it to disappear completely, leaving her face in its natural condition. Mrs. King was from Portage des Sioux, a village thirteen miles from St. Charles, and the story of her wonderful cure is one of the traditions connected with the name of the holy Mother.

Twenty years later, the little oratory needed repairs, and it was thought advisable to ascertain the condition of the remains. This time, nothing was found but a considerable part of the bones, and a quantity of ashes. These were transferred with all the ceremonies appointed by the Church for such occasions, to an iron coffer, about a yard in length, which was placed in the vault under the floor of the oratory, June 13, 1876.

The third exhumation took place on January 28, 1896, on the occasion of the canonical authentication of the remains, which was to close the Ordinary Process, begun in St. Louis, in May, 1895. They were found just as they were when placed in the iron coffer twenty years previously, except that the latter was full to the brim of water as pure as if it had been distilled. This water was drained off and carefully kept; and by the use of it several cures were obtained, one of them a case of tuberculosis in its last stage. After the ceremony, the remains were restored to their resting place as before. A fourth exhumation will take place at the close of the Apostolic Process begun at Rome in April of 1911.

By the approbation of the Ordinary Process, and the regular introduction of her cause, December 8, 1909, Mother Duchesne became entitled to the appellation of the Venerable Servant of God, Philippine Duchesne.

A few words before closing, concerning the work of Venerable Mother Duchesne. We have seen that she had personally founded six houses, three in Missouri and three in Louisiana, and also that the mission among the Pottowatomies, was due in a great measure to her prayers and exertions. Just at the time of this last foundation, the Society of the Sacred Heart entered upon a period of rapid expansion, and when the venerable Mother died, ten years later, it already counted sixteen houses in the United States and Canada; while now, there are twenty-seven in the former country, and five in the latter. But the great tree, of which Mother Duchesne was the vigorous root, spread its branches still further. For she it was who had enkindled the sacred fire of the apostolic spirit in the heart of Mother du Rousier who, in the designs of God, was to be the pioneer of the Sacred Heart in the vast regions of South America.

CHAPTER IX

SOME FRUITS OF HER WORK

When Mother Duchesne with her companions, was on her way to Bordeaux to take passage for the New World, she stopped at the convent of Poitiers. There, as everywhere, her enterprise excited the deepest interest and admiration. The children were, of course, eager to see and hear her; and, in the youthful crowd that gathered around her full of expectancy, there was one child, not yet in her 'teens, broad-browed, and with eyes full of earnest thoughtfulness. As she listened to the burning words of the missionary, she caught the glow of her holy enthusiasm, and felt that she too would one day be called to follow in her footsteps. This child was Anna du Rousier. When next she saw Mother Duchesne, it was at the deathbed of the latter, as already related. When she came to America, it was with the understanding that, after giving a year to the visitation of the houses of the Society, she would proceed to South America, and see how conditions were in various places of that part of the world, where foundations had been asked for. It can not be doubted that she earnestly recommended her future mission to Mother Duchesne, and received from her a fervent promise that she would intercede for it. The year following her deathbed interview with the saintly Mother she received orders to set out for Santiago de Chili under the guidance and protection of a small company of Chilian priests bound for that city, and to begin a foundation there. When this order reached her, God permitted that she should be seized with so violent a repugnance for this mission that, though she did not for a moment think of offering any objections, it was only after spending an entire night on her knees before the Blessed Sacrament, in agonized struggles and supplications to her Divine Master, that He stilled the tempest of temptation, and gave her the victory. Mother du Rousier was a character of heroic type, worthy of a place beside even such women as Mother Barat and her great daughter, Mother Duchesne. It was after a long and dangerous journey, with Mother Mary McNally, an American professed from the New York Vicariate, and one lay sister, that she reached her destination, and began the foundation at Santiago in 1853. At her death in 1880, two years after celebrating its silver jubilee, she left five houses, four in Chili and one in Peru, while a sixth was in preparation in the city of Buenos Aires. At the present time there are two Vicariates on the South American continent, and a house at Bogota, in the Republic of Colombia.

We have still to speak of two other offshoots, sprung from the same root as the North and South American Vicariates. These are the Vicariates of Mexico and Oceania. The former is due, under the direction of the Superior General of the Society, to the enterprise and devotedness of the then Vicar of Louisiana, Reverend Mother Elizabeth Moran, at that time residing in Grand

Coteau, Mother Duchesne's second foundation, of which she had been a pupil. With a few companions from her own Vicariate, she began the foundation of Mexico in 1882. About seventeen years later when she was removed to another field of labor, she left behind her a fully organized Vicariate comprising eight houses, including two in Havana and one in Puerto Rico, all founded by herself except the boarding-school of Havana, which was the work of that other great religious, Mother Aloysia Hardey, who was herself a pupil of Grand Coteau, and the foundress of most of the Eastern houses of the Society.

Perhaps the most remarkable of the Religious of the Sacred Heart trained by Mother Duchesne in person, was Mother Anna Shannon, who was such a power in Louisiana, especially during the Civil War. She was then in charge of the Vice-Vicariate of Louisiana and resided in St. Michael's, while not far away, also fronting the Mississippi River, stood the old-time Jefferson College, which the calamities of the time had closed. The war was not yet over when it was reopened by a band of French Marist Fathers, invited by Bishop Odin, and Madame Shannon, as she was generally called, with the warmhearted liberality that characterized her, gave them every assistance in her power. They became the chaplains of the convent, and were the kindest of neighbors. Ten or twelve years later, Father Chataignier, one of the Fathers who had reopened the college, was engaged in missionary work in New Zealand. Having been consulted by Archbishop Redwood of Wellington, as to the religious Congregation to which it would be advisable to entrust the academy for girls he wished to found in his diocese, the good Father at once proposed the Society of the Sacred Heart. The negotiations which followed resulted in the foundation of Timaru, made in person by Reverend Mother Suzanna Boudreau, who had also been educated at Grand Coteau, and had succeeded Reverend Mother Anna Shannon as Vicar of Louisiana. At this time, however, she was in charge of the Vicariate of the West and toward the end of 1879 she set out with a little band of her own daughters, for the first foundation of the Society of the Sacred Heart in Oceania. Mother Boudreau was to have returned to St. Louis as soon as it was organized; but early in the following year, an acute laryngitis carried her off in a few days. This sorrowful event placed the stamp of the cross upon the new-born foundation, which has since grown into a Vicariate of ten houses, including the two recently established day schools in Japan, at Tokio and Kobe.

Sixty years have gone by since Venerable Mother Duchesne was laid away to rest, close to the old "Rock Church" adjoining the convent of St. Charles; but she still lives in the memory of the people among whom she toiled, and prayed, and suffered. In the convent, the staircase that cut off a large corner of her cell has been removed to another place; and that narrow little room, still known as "Mother Duchesne's Cell," has been converted into a sanctuary in which are kept all the mementoes of the holy mother, which have not found their way elsewhere. Conspicuous among those remaining at the convent, is the picture of St. Francis Régis, which in fulfillment of a vow, she had placed above the altar of the Church at Florissant. In the community, her virtues are still recalled, and her actions recounted. The little oratory in the front garden, often sees the religious on their knees in prayer, beside her tomb, and it is likewise piously frequented by people of the town, and of the neighboring country, as also by pilgrims from St. Louis and elsewhere. Her name is a household word among the Catholics of Missouri, and her pupils and their descendants have borne it with them, wherever the vicissitudes of life have carried them. Even the remnants of the Pottowatomie tribe, now located in the Indian Territory, still speak with veneration of "The woman who prays always," whom it was the happiness of their grandfathers to have known. She is one of the traditions of the country, and has left a stamp upon it so strongly marked that even the casual traveler, if at all observant, can not fail to notice it. Catholic France has had a very considerable share in the upbuilding of the Catholic Church in this country, through the labors of so many heroic missionaries whom she sent out to us, even in the midst of her struggles against persecution at home. And among the many gifts by which she has acquired a title to the gratitude of American Catholics, one of the greatest was the Venerable Philippine Duchesne.

Milton Keynes UK
Ingram Content Group UK Ltd.
UKHW031301251024
450245UK00004B/388